D0626815

Revised & Updated Edition

The Gifted Kids' Survival Guide

For Ages 10 & Under

Judy Galbraith, M.A.

The Gifted Kids' Survival Guide

For Ages 10 & Under

Judy Galbraith, M.A.

Edited by Pamela Espeland

free spirit
PUBLiSHiNG®

Works
for kids™

Library of Congress Cataloging-in-Publication Data

Galbraith, Judy
    The gifted kids' survival guide, for ages 10 & under / by Judy
Galbraith ; edited by Pamela Espeland ; illustrated by Albert
Molnar. — Rev. and expanded ed.
        p.   cm.
    Includes bibliographical references and index.
    Summary: Examines the problems of gifted and talented students
and explains how they can make the best use of their educational
opportunities, get along better with parents and friends, and better
understand themselves.
      ISBN 1-57542-053-8
      1. Gifted children—Education (Elementary)—Juvenile literature.
2. Gifted children—Juvenile literature.   [1. Gifted children.]
I. Espeland, Pamela. 1951–   . II. Molnar, Albert, ill.
III. Title.
LC3993.22.G35   1999
371.95–dc21   98-41344
                                                       CIP
                                                        AC

10 9 8 7 6 5 4 3 2 1
Printed in the United States of America

Cover design by Circus Design
Page design and typesetting by Percolator
Interior illustrations by Albert Molnar and Marieka Heinlen
Index compiled by Diana Witt

Free Spirit Publishing Inc.
400 First Avenue North, Suite 616
Minneapolis, MN 55401-1724
(612) 338-2068
help4kids@freespirit.com
http://www.freespirit.com

Dedication

To my mother…for giving me a good mind, and for raising me in a home where I was expected to use it well.

To my father…for teaching me to appreciate the wilderness (no matter how bad the weather), and for showing me the value of trying new things.

Acknowledgments

Many heartfelt thanks to Kate Benson for meticulously tabulating the survey results and commenting on the manuscript for this book. Her enthusiastic and insightful help was much appreciated.

Hundreds of students participated in the surveys for this book, and their responses were very important to its development. I'm grateful for their thoughts, advice, and ideas.

My editor, confidant, and true friend Pamela Espeland is a gifted writer *and* a great advocate for gifted kids. Her excellent writing skills and genuine interest in this book were essential to its creation.

Contents

QUICK QUIZ!

	Yes	No
1. Is your schoolwork mostly easy for you to do?	☐	☐
2. Do you usually finish ahead of others in your class?	☐	☐
3. Do you hate it when you're not allowed to work ahead?	☐	☐
4. Are you in a special class or program at your school?	☐	☐
5. Do you ever get teased or picked on for being smart, weird, or nerdy?	☐	☐
6. Are you good at a lot of different things?	☐	☐
7. Do you like being challenged at school?	☐	☐
8. When you think about things no one else thinks of, do you wonder why your brain works the way it does?	☐	☐
9. Do your parents and teachers expect you to get straight A's?	☐	☐
10. Has anyone ever said "If you're so smart, why didn't you . . . (ace the test, know the answer, get everything right, etc.)?"	☐	☐

SCORING: If you answered YES to some, most, or all of these questions, this book is for you.

From *The Gifted Kids' Survival Guide For Ages 10 & Under* by Judy Galbraith, M.A., © 1999. Free Spirit Publishing Inc., Minneapolis, MN; 800/735/7323. This page may be photocopied for individual or small group use only.

About This Book

The Gifted Kids' Survival Guide was written with help from hundreds of GTs* who took part in surveys, wrote letters, asked questions, gave opinions, and talked to me when I visited their schools and classrooms. (A BIG thanks to all of you, your teachers, and your parents.)

In addition to being gifted, those kids (like you) have questions about what being gifted means, why they think and learn the way they do, how to make school more challenging, how to make friends, how to cope with teasing, and more. This book has answers you're looking for, plus things to think about and ideas to try. It won't answer *all* of your questions or solve *all* of your problems, but it will help with some of the hassles that give you grief.

GTs have told me that when they know more about giftedness, they feel better about themselves. And when you feel good about who you are, you're in the best position to be your own person and make the most of your talents and abilities.

This book was written *for* you, not *about* you. Read it front to back, back to front, or skip around. It's YOUR book.

---

* Many gifted kids have said they don't like the label "gifted." Some prefer words like "smart," "intelligent," or "talented." Most would rather be called "Jon" or "Amanda" or "Carlos" or "Kareem" or "Mai" or whatever their real names are. I don't like labels either, but using "GT" in this book simplifies things. It stands for "Gifted and Talented," but you can decide it means whatever you want ... Gargantuan Thinker? Great Talker? Galaxy Traveler?

What About This Book?

Tell me what you think about *The Gifted Kids' Survival Guide* when you're through reading it (or while you're reading it). You can write to me:

Judy Galbraith
Free Spirit Publishing Inc.
400 First Avenue North, Suite 616
Minneapolis, MN 55401-1724

If you're online, you can email me:
help4kids@freespirit.com

Or drop me a note at the Free Spirit Web site:
http://www.freespirit.com

P.S. I LOVE getting letters from readers, and I ALWAYS answer them!

8 Great Gripes of Gifted Kids

According to surveys, letters, and GTs I've talked to, here are the eight *worst* things about being gifted:

1. We miss out on some classes and activities other kids get to do.

2. We have to do extra work in school.

3. We get teased for being smart.

4. Other kids ask us for too much help.

5. The stuff we do in school is too easy and it's boring.

6. When we finish our schoolwork early, we often can't work ahead.

7. Our friends and classmates don't always understand us.

8. Parents, teachers, and even our friends expect too much of us. We're supposed to get A's and do our best all the time.

Do you have gripes that aren't on this list? Write them here:

_____

_____

_____

_____

According to surveys, letters, and GTs I've talked to, here are the eight *best* things about being gifted:

1. Our schoolwork in GT classes is more challenging and we learn more.

2. We get to do special things—activities, field trips, and projects.

3. Schoolwork is easy for us to understand.

4. When we're in special programs and classes, we meet new people and get to be with friends who understand us.

5. We can help others.

6. Our friends and other kids look up to us.

7. We like being smart. It feels good.

8. We look forward to a better future.

Do you know great things that aren't on this list? Write them here:

_____

_____

_____

_____

GTs Speak Out:
What's bad and good about being GT?

What's BAD?

 "Being teased."
—Boys and girls, ages 7–12

 "People expect more of you than they do of others your age."*—Girl, 10*

 "Some kids are jealous and are snobby to me."*—Girl, 9*

 "Having to make up regular class work."*—Girl, 9½*

 "The NERDY NICKNAMES."
—Girl, 10

What's GOOD?

 "You get to leave the regular class and learn cool things."—*Boys and girls, ages 7–12*

 "You get work done faster, and you catch onto ideas faster."—*Girl, 12*

 "You can help your friends with something they need help on."—*Girl, 9*

 "You get treated more maturely."—*Girl, 10*

 "Being in a smaller class."—*Girl, 8*

 "You know you can do anything if you put your mind to it."—*Boy, 12*

When Did You Know?

Some GTs know they're gifted soon after they start school (or even earlier). Their parents might have told them. Their teachers might have told them. Or they might have figured out for themselves that they aren't quite like many other kids their age.

> "Most gifted children know they are different by the time they are five."
>
> —Dr. Philip Powell

Many GTs don't know they're gifted until they're accepted into a special program for the gifted and talented. Even then, some aren't sure, because often these programs aren't called "gifted programs." Why not? Because some adults aren't comfortable with that language. They worry that if certain kids are labeled "gifted," they might get conceited. Or that kids who aren't labeled "gifted" might feel bad. So don't be fooled if your program is called...

AIM   PEAK
Advanced Learner   REACH
Autonomous Learner   SAGE
Exceptional Student   SEARCH
DELTA   STAR
GATE   TAG

...or some other name. No matter what they're called, these programs have the same purpose: *To challenge students who need more stimulation than the regular coursework or classroom teachers can provide.*

Most GTs who are selected for special programs are happy about it. They enjoy the challenge. They love learning new things. They like to learn at a faster pace with other kids who can keep up with them. Especially if they've been feeling bored and restless in regular classes, they're amazed to discover that LEARNING IS FUN.

But they still have questions like:

"What does it mean to be gifted?"

"Why am I gifted? How did I get this way?"

"How was I picked for this class?"

"Why wasn't my friend picked? He/she gets good grades, too."

"Does being gifted mean I should get straight A's all the time?"

"Does it mean I have a high IQ?"

"Does it mean I'm weird?"

"Does it mean I'll automatically be a good dancer, artist, or musician?"

"Does it mean I'm supposed to be good at everything?"

"Does it mean I'm better than everyone else?"

"Does it mean I can't ever make mistakes?"

Adults don't always tell you what you want to know about being GT. They're afraid you might feel too different from other kids—at a time when most kids want to fit in.

But they're wrong. Dead wrong.

When GTs find out about giftedness, they feel GREAT!

Chances are you've always known that you think and learn differently from many kids. Your friends know it, too; that's why they say things like "You're so smart" or "You always do everything right." But that's not enough. You want to know MORE.

Being labeled "gifted," "talented," or "high potential" is a start. Labels are a pain, but they're part of life. They help us to understand and communicate concepts and ideas.

Except when people can't agree on what they mean.

Except when you're stuck with TOO MANY LABELS.

GTs Speak Out:
How do you feel about being called "gifted"?

 "It depends on how it is being used. If someone is giving me a compliment, I like it. But if someone is making fun of me, I don't."—*Boy, 11*

 "Sometimes I don't like it because it makes me feel different but I am just like them."—*Girl, 10*

 "I feel proud."—*Boy, 10*

 "I don't like being called gifted that much. I just like being called my regular name."
—*Boy, 9*

"I feel as if a lot of people depend on me to know answers, but other than that I like being called 'gifted.'"—*Girl, 9*

 "I feel great, but I don't like to show it."—*Boy, 10*

 "It kind of makes me feel out of place."—*Girl, 9*

 "It feels great! I feel people know that I'm smarter than the average bear."—*Girl, 10*

 "It's kind of a compliment but I don't like it when the teachers say 'he's very high potential' all of the time."—*Boy, 10 ½*

 "I feel happy because my parents are proud of me, but other times I feel embarrassed when people ask me 'Where are you going?' and 'What is REACH?'"—*Girl, 10*

De-fə-'ni-shəns

FACT #1:
"Gifted" means different things
to different people.

Here's how *Webster's Collegiate Dictionary* defines it:

> 1: having great natural ability : talented (~ children)
> 2: revealing a special gift (~ voices).

The National Association for Gifted Children explains it this way:

> Someone who shows, or has the potential for showing, an exceptional
> level of performance in one or more areas of expression.

TAGFAM (Families of the Gifted and Talented) uses this definition:

> *Intellectual giftedness* (n.) — Mental quickness and mental
> flexibility arising from heredity and influenced by environment.

Psychologist Lewis Terman defined it in terms of the Stanford-Binet
Intelligence Scale (which he helped to create), saying:

> The top one percent level in general intelligence ability as measured
> by the Stanford-Binet Intelligence Scale or a comparable instrument.

And here's what the U.S. Office of Education came up with:

> **Gifted and talented children are those identified by professionally qualified persons who by virtue of outstanding abilities are capable of high performance.**

Are you confused yet? Take a deep breath, because that's not all.

FACT #2:
There are many different ways of being gifted.

ACADEMIC ABILITY. Kids may be gifted in one or more subjects: math, reading, social studies, spelling, science, music, art, or physical education. (Many GTs are more challenged when they're *ability grouped* in school, so they can learn new things instead of waiting for others to catch up. Some GTs are moved ahead a grade or two in certain subjects because they're ready for that level.)

THINK ABOUT IT: What classes seem to come naturally when you put your mind to work on them?

CREATIVE THINKING. Highly creative kids are good at thinking up unusual ways to solve tough problems. They may have wild and crazy ways of doing things. They may be clever and good at thinking up jokes. Creative people are different, and they like it that way! (Sometimes adults have a hard time accepting very creative kids, who often question why things are done the way they are. Creatively gifted people enjoy bending or breaking rules, and this makes many adults feel uneasy.)

THINK ABOUT IT: Have you ever come up with a way to do your math problems that's faster than the way your teacher taught you?

VISUAL/PERFORMING ARTS. Talented performers are considered gifted in a special way. They express themselves best through art, dance, drama, or music. They're normally very creative and flexible, and they like to show their stuff.

THINK ABOUT IT: Do you know anyone who fits this description? What's his or her special talent? Do you have a special talent?

LEADERSHIP. People with leadership ability are excellent decision makers. They like to take responsibility, and they have high expectations for themselves and others. They're popular, self-confident, and good at motivating people.

THINK ABOUT IT: Are you the kind of person who's organized and likes to tell other people what to do?

GENERAL INTELLECTUAL ABILITY. Kids with this kind of giftedness are smart in many ways. They get excited about new ideas, learn quickly, use a large vocabulary, ask a lot of questions, and enjoy abstract, complex thinking.

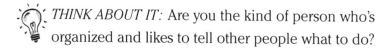 *THINK ABOUT IT:* Are you a superfast learner? Do your friends sometimes think you're stuck up because you use big words? Do you know a lot about many different things? Are you a self-starter?

FACT #3:
Most people DO agree about one thing when it comes to giftedness.

When you're gifted, you have HIGH POTENTIAL. When you have HIGH POTENTIAL, this means your brain has the power to help you achieve great things *if you try.*

At some point in your life, your teachers or parents might have said "You're not working up to your potential." But what if you're doing all of your schoolwork, even finishing early?

And you're getting good grades?

And you're not acting out in class?

??! What do they WANT ?!? from you?

The answer is: They know you're capable of MORE. Much more. You can go far beyond the regular schoolwork—or even the GT program—*if you try.* It's up to adults to give you opportunities, but it's up to YOU to take them.

You've heard the old saying "You can lead a horse to water, but you can't make him drink." If your teachers are challenging you, if your parents are encouraging you to explore new things, say yes. (Unless you're already way too busy, but that's another topic. See pages 75–76.)

You could be the smartest person in the world, but if you don't use your HIGH POTENTIAL, you might as well have a pea brain.

FACT #4:
Most GTs share one or more of the following characteristics.

Teachers who select kids for special programs look for students who:

✔ learn easily and quickly
✔ are persistent—if they don't succeed, they try, try again
✔ ask a lot of questions and are very curious
✔ have a good sense of humor
✔ dislike doing the same thing over and over and over and over and over and over and over…
✔ are very sensitive toward others
✔ think logically and want things to make sense
✔ are open to new and zany ideas.

THINK ABOUT IT: How many of these characteristics do you have?

P.S. It's mind-boggling to think of the different ways people can be gifted…and I haven't even listed all the ways. It's easy to get frustrated trying to figure it all out. RELAX. There are no right or wrong answers. There are just different ways of defining giftedness.

GTs Speak Out:
What does "gifted" mean to you?

 "Being above grade level and smart."—*Girl, 10*

 "I can understand and learn things faster than other kids."—*Girl, 10*

 "It means you've got special ways about you."—*Girl, 9*

 "Being smart and using it."—*Boy, 9*

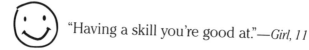 "Having a skill you're good at."—*Girl, 11*

"It means you have reached terminal brain velocity, and you deserve to be in a special class."—*Boy, 8*

 "Being creative, intelligent, and talented."—*Girl, 11*

 "It means you might become someone popular and rich."—*Boy, 10*

 "It means you need higher challenges in school."—*Boy, 12*

 "It means being able to problem solve and troubleshoot."—*Girl, 10¾*

 "It means you think on your own."—*Boy, 9*

"All it means to me is that I learn a little faster than other kids but I still have normal friends and I'm not a NERD!"—*Girl, 10*

What's Your Definition?

What does "gifted" mean to you?

_____

_____

_____

_____

_____

_____

_____

_____

_____

Even more important…. How can you use your giftedness to make life more fun, interesting, and meaningful? What will you do with your HIGH POTENTIAL?

_____

_____

_____

_____

_____

_____

_____

_____

Multiple Intelligences

What if we stop trying to define "giftedness" and start trying to define "intelligence"? Howard Gardner, a psychologist at the Harvard School of Education, has been doing that for the past several years. He believes that the brain contains at least *eight* different intelligences. Dr. Gardner's ideas have made many people think about how kids learn (and how teachers should teach).

Here are the intelligences Dr. Gardner has come up with . . . so far. Which ones do you have?

LINGUISTIC INTELLIGENCE. People with this kind of intelligence have an easy time using and understanding language. They enjoy reading, writing, talking, and s-p-e-l-l-i-n-g. They may be great storytellers.

LOOK AHEAD: If you have this type of intelligence, you might grow up to be a writer, editor, novelist, poet, public speaker, speechwriter, reporter, lawyer, researcher, publicist, or "Webmeister."

LOGICAL-MATHEMATICAL INTELLIGENCE. People with this kind of intelligence have an easy time with numbers and math concepts. They often enjoy science. They love games, riddles, and computers.

LOOK AHEAD: If you have this type of intelligence, you might grow up to be an astronaut, astronomer, engineer, lawyer, police investigator, pharmacist, architect, detective, chemist, analyst, statistician, physicist, accountant, computer programmer, software developer, meteorologist, or inventor.

VISUAL-SPATIAL INTELLIGENCE. People with this kind of intelligence understand how objects and figures relate in three-dimensional space. *Examples:* They can tell when a building isn't quite symmetrical. They can judge the angle needed to score a goal in hockey or a basket in basketball. They can rotate complex forms in their heads and look at them from all sides. They're good at taking things apart and putting them back together, and they love games, puzzles, and maps.

LOOK AHEAD: If you have this type of intelligence, you might grow up to be an artist (painter, sculptor, etc.), architect, filmmaker, navigator, Web page designer, game designer, chess player, advertising executive, clothing or costume designer, construction worker, animator, interior decorator, photojournalist, mechanic, graphic designer, or commercial artist.

MUSICAL-RHYTHMIC INTELLIGENCE. People with this kind of intelligence understand music, rhythms, patterns, tempos, and sounds. They easily hear tone and pitch, and they may be good at playing one or more musical instruments—with training or by ear. They love all kinds of music.

LOOK AHEAD: If you have this type of intelligence, you might grow up to be a musician, band or orchestra director or member, songwriter, poet, DJ, composer, singer, or music teacher.

BODILY-KINESTHETIC INTELLIGENCE. People with this kind of intelligence move their bodies with grace and ease. They enjoy training their bodies to be strong, flexible, and capable. They're good at handling and manipulating objects, and they excel at crafts—carving, sewing, weaving, making pots. They can be great mimics.

LOOK AHEAD: If you have this type of intelligence, you might grow up to be a dancer, actor, surgeon, comedian, professional athlete, fitness instructor, gymnast, sports trainer, coach, team manager, physical therapist, karate instructor, mechanic, or craftsperson.

INTERPERSONAL INTELLIGENCE. People with this kind of intelligence are good at understanding others and their feelings. They're natural leaders and mediators.

INTRAPERSONAL INTELLIGENCE. People with this kind of intelligence understand themselves very well—much better than others might understand them. They're aware of their feelings, dreams, and ideas. They set goals for themselves and reach them. They enjoy keeping journals.

LOOK AHEAD: If you have either type of personal intelligence (inter- or intra-), you might grow up to be a teacher, psychologist, counselor, youth leader, salesperson, doctor, nurse, special educator, social worker, child care specialist, school principal, politician, president, entrepreneur, philosopher, detective, librarian, paralegal, law enforcer, writer, poet, or religious leader.

NATURALIST INTELLIGENCE. People with this kind of intelligence feel a deep connection to the natural world, plants, and animals. They love being outdoors. They're great gardeners and/or cooks. They understand how things fit into categories.

LOOK AHEAD: If you have this type of intelligence, you might grow up to be a park ranger, botanist, zoologist, zookeeper, chef, farmer, veterinarian, DNR official, gardener, landscaper, commercial fisherman (or woman), environmental activist, or florist.

Here's another way to understand multiple intelligences: Not all GTs get straight A's. Not all kids who get straight A's are GT. That's because people have different intelligences.

You may be strong in one subject and not so strong in others. You may be *really* good at math and not so good at art, science, or reading. You might be a *great* artist and a total disaster at math. It depends on which intelligences you have and which ones you don't have—or haven't yet developed.

> "There are hundreds and hundreds of ways to succeed, and many, many different abilities that will help you get there."
>
> —Howard Gardner

5 Things You Need to Succeed

No matter what gifts or intelligences you have, you need these things to reach your HIGH POTENTIAL:

1. Challenge. You need people, schoolwork, classes, activities, and opportunities that will S-T-R-E-T-C-H your mind.

2. Self-esteem. You need to feel pleased and proud of the person you are—just the way you are. This doesn't mean you can't or shouldn't try to be even better. But you need to believe in your own basic worth.

> **IMPORTANT:** No one can give you self-esteem; no one can take your self-esteem away. It's up to YOU. And the way you build self-esteem is by *doing things that make you feel pleased and proud of the person you are.*

3. Communication. You need people to talk to. Peers who understand you. Teachers, parents, and other adults who will listen. Opportunities to tell other people what you think and how you feel. Chances to ask questions. *Tip:* Writing is a great way to communicate. It helps you to organize your thinking and express yourself clearly. A great way to communicate with *yourself* is to keep a journal.

4. Self-awareness. You need to know yourself. What are your strengths and weaknesses? Your hopes and dreams? Who ARE you, anyway? If you don't know, how can you find out? Can you start asking yourself questions? What do you think? (GET IT?)

5. Help. You need people in your life who are willing to help you. People you can turn to with questions and problems. People who want the best for you. Make a list of people you can count on for help. Will you list your parents? Brother(s) or sister(s)? Teachers? Friends? Who else?

GT Programs: Who Gets In?

Most of the time, teachers or other school officials choose GTs for special programs or classes. They often base their recommendations on several measurements including:

✔ achievement test scores,
✔ IQ scores,
✔ teacher recommendations, and
✔ parent recommendations.

Achievement Test Scores

Achievement test scores tell how well you're learning things you are taught in school. The tests measure your progress in math, reading, science, social studies, and other school subjects.

You remember what those tests are all about: STOP! PUT YOUR PENCILS DOWN! DO NOT TURN TO THE NEXT PAGE UNTIL YOU ARE TOLD TO DO SO! Blah, blah, blah.

Your scores will probably be a little different in each area, because not all GTs are good at everything. But if you're chosen for a GT program, it's likely your scores are tops in more than one subject. In fact, many GTs' achievement test scores show them working at least *two years beyond* what kids their age normally do.

P.S. Achievement tests have names. Some of the most commonly used tests are:

Iowa Test of Basic Skills • Comprehensive Test of Basic Skills • Stanford Achievement Test • Scholastic Assessment Test • National Assessment of Educational Progress • Metropolitan Achievement Test • National Achievement Test

IQ Scores

IQ is the abbreviation for Intelligence Quotient. In simple terms, that's a score of how well you can accomplish school-type intellectual tasks. If your IQ is high, you have the potential to do very well in school. (Whether you *do* is up to you.)

"You should use your talent because if you don't it's just like not having it."

—Doug, 9

The average IQ is 100. Anything over 100 is above average (it doesn't take a genius to figure that out). Here's how other scores are rated—and about how many people have those scores:

IQ Score	Classification	About How Many People?
160	Very superior	1 in 10,000
150	Very superior	9 in 10,000
140	Very superior	7 in 1,000
130	Superior	3 in 100
120	Superior	11 in 100
110	Bright	27 in 100

What IQ scores *don't* show is how creative you are. Or what kind of athlete or musician or leader you could be. Or whether or not you have the motivation to use your GT brain. That's why it's important for adults to look at other things and not just IQ scores when they pick kids for gifted classes.

Check It Out! ··

A score of 132 on the Stanford-Binet Intelligence Scale qualifies you for membership in Mensa, the International High IQ Society. Mensans range in age from 4 to 94, but most are between 20 and 49. In education, they range from preschoolers to high school dropouts to people with several Ph.Ds. To find out more, write, call, or visit the Web site:

American Mensa
1229 Corporate Drive West
Arlington, TX 76006-6103
(817) 649-5232
1-800-66MENSA (1-800-666-3672)
http://www.mensa.org/

Teacher or Parent Recommendations

When parents or teachers recommend kids for special GT programs or classes, they usually put it in writing. They write their perceptions and feelings about the students' abilities. Sometimes the school gives them a checklist that tells them what to watch for. *Examples:*

✔ Does the student ask a lot of questions?
✔ Does the student have lots of information on many things?
✔ Does the student understand easily?
✔ Does the student enjoy solving puzzles and problems?
✔ Does the student have a zany sense of humor?

Students who have many of the qualities described in the checklist are likely candidates for GT programs.

But even with checklists and test scores to help them decide who's GT, teachers and parents can make mistakes.

Believe It . . . or Not!

Many famous GTs were misjudged when they were in school. You might be surprised to learn that . . .

Lucille Ball (*I Love Lucy* star) was an aspiring actress when the head of a drama school advised her to "try another profession. *Any* other."

Beethoven (composer) had a music teacher who described him as "hopeless."

Winston Churchill (English Prime Minister) failed sixth grade and finished last in his class at Harrow, England.

Charles Darwin (*Origin of the Species* author) failed a medical course at Edinburgh University. His father once told him "You will be a disgrace to yourself and all your family."

Thomas Edison (inventor) was told by his teachers that he was too stupid to learn anything.

Albert Einstein (Nobel Prize-winning physicist) performed so poorly in high school that a teacher asked him to drop out, saying "You will never amount to anything, Einstein."

Dr. Robert Jarvick (artificial heart inventor) was rejected by 15 American medical schools.

Michael Jordan (Chicago Bulls star) got beat out for North Carolina High School Player of the Year. His teachers told him to go into math, "where the money is."

John F. Kennedy (35th U.S. President) received constant reports of "poor achievement" in school and was a lousy speller.

Diana Nyad (champion swimmer) was kicked out of college.

Paul Orfalea (Kinko's founder) was placed in a class for retarded students after he failed second grade. (He has dyslexia.)

Orville Wright (aviation pioneer) was expelled from sixth grade.

GT Programs: Who Might Get Left Out?

The selection process for GT programs doesn't always work the way it should. It isn't always fair. Some people who should get in are left out. *Examples:*

Girls

This is a bigger problem in middle school and high school than it is in elementary school. By the upper grades, many gifted girls have learned to hide their abilities so they can fit in and feel "normal." (Read more about gifted girls on pages 56–57.)

Boys with a Lot of Energy

Many young boys have a tough time sitting still in class and doing paper-and-pencil work. Some are so energetic that they are (wrongly) believed to have ADD (Attention Deficit Disorder). (Read more about gifted boys on pages 58–59.)

Kids with Disabilities

Some kids have physical, emotional, or learning disabilities that make it hard to show their GT-ness in "normal" ways. (Researcher Nick Colangelo has found that when teachers and parent groups are asked to imagine a "gifted child," they almost never picture one with disabilities.)

Troublemakers

Some teachers think that "good" behavior = GT and "bad" behavior = not GT. Rock star Roger Daltrey (lead singer for The Who) was expelled from his grammar school in England. "I was an evil little so-and-so," he remembers. "I didn't fit in."

Kids from Minority Cultures

Many standardized achievement tests and IQ tests are biased in favor of white middle- to upper-class students. They don't do a good job of measuring the skills and abilities of kids from minority cultures or families where English is a second language.

Kids from Low-Income Families

Kids whose families are struggling have a lot to worry about. Their gifts might not be obvious. And if they change schools a lot—or, even worse, are homeless—they can usually forget about getting into GT programs.

Kids Who Don't Do Well on Tests

Some GTs simply aren't good at taking tests. The test situation may be too stressful for them. Or they may have personal problems that keep them from concentrating. Either way, their scores don't show what they really know.

"Test scores should never 'define' a person, no matter what they may reveal about his or her intellectual or achievement potential. . . . All tests are imperfect measurers."

—Jean Peterson

Kids Who Are Smart but Not Necessarily GT

What's the difference? This might help:*

Smart Kids	GTs
know the answers	ask the questions
are interested	are very curious
pay attention	get involved mentally and physically
work hard	play around and still get good grades and test scores
answer questions	question answers
enjoy same-age peers	prefer adults or older children
are good at memorizing	are good at guessing
learn easily	are bored; already know the answers
listen well	show strong feelings and opinions
are self-satisfied	are highly critical of themselves (perfectionists)

* From "The Gifted and Talented Child," Maryland Council for Gifted & Talented Children, Inc., P.O. Box 12221, Silver Spring, MD 20908.

More De-fə-'ni-shəns

These words and phrases will come in handy if you're in (or in the running for) your school's GT program:

Stanford-Binet: A type of intelligence test. It scores verbal, non-verbal, mathematical reasoning, and short-term memory.

Cluster Classes: Placing GTs in a special class or together in a group in the regular classroom.

Compacted Courses: A number of courses compressed into one.

Continuous Progress: Students progress according to ability rather than grade level.

Early Entrance: Entrance into school before the usual entrance age or date.

Grade Skipping: Advancing or accelerating GTs through grades ahead of the usual age or date.

Magnet School: A school for GTs or students with a special interest area (Spanish, the arts, etc.).

Mentorship: Students are linked with a teacher, parent, or older student who acts as a friend, a guide, and a coach.

Pull-Out Program: Students are pulled from classes for an hour or more each week for extension or enrichment study.

WISC III: A type of intelligence test. The Verbal Scale measures verbal expression and comprehension. The Performance Scale measures areas such as spatial relationships.

Reprinted with permission from GT World, 1998. *www.gtworld.org*

GTs Speak Out:
What's good and bad about GT programs?

What's GOOD?

 "I like not being bored."—*Girl, 9*

 "I like working on special projects and independent studies."—*Boy, 9*

 "I like working at my level with others at my level."—*Boy, 12*

 "The work we do is challenging and we get to work at our own pace."—*Girl, 12*

 "I like how my teacher makes it fun to learn."—*Girl, 9*

What's BAD?

 "I don't like the work we have to make up when we miss class."—*Boys and girls, ages 7–12*

 "I don't like being teased about it." —*Boys and girls, ages 7–12*

 "I don't like having to miss recess." —*Boys and girls, ages 7–12*

"Sometimes I feel like all we do is work, work, work."—*Boy, 11*

 "I don't like being away from my friends in the regular class."—*Boy, 8*

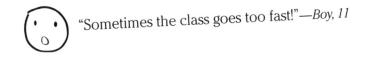 "Sometimes the class goes too fast!"—*Boy, 11*

What If There's No GT Program?

More and more, schools are eliminating special programs for GTs. Instead, they're focusing on "providing a challenging level of academic study for all children." Parents who ask about gifted programs might be told "All of our children are gifted."

This sounds good, but don't believe it. All children are *not* gifted. Saying they are doesn't make it so. It's kind of like saying "All of our children have 20/20 vision" when some, in fact, need glasses or they can't see the board.

In schools without GT programs:

✔ Teachers and administrators might not know much about giftedness.

✔ Gifted children aren't identified.

✔ GTs might not get the challenges and opportunities they need and deserve.

In some states, gifted education is *mandated,* meaning that schools are required by law to identify and/or provide services for gifted students. In others, gifted education is *discretionary,* meaning that schools are *allowed* but not required to do anything special for gifted students.

If your school doesn't have a GT program, talk to your parents. Talk to teachers who believe that GTs should be challenged at school. There's not much *you* can do to change things, but you might be able to motivate adults who can.

YRUGT?

I don't need to tell you that giftedness has nothing to do with gifts. No one is *given* high intelligence, creativity, athletic skills, or leadership ability.

But every GT has at least one pair of *designer genes*. In other words, some of your giftedness is inherited, which means one or both of your parents are GT, too. Or maybe you inherited your giftedness from a grandparent or other close relative.

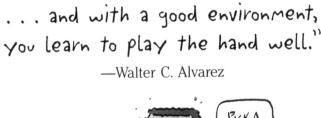

"With a good heredity, nature deals you a fine hand at cards . . .

Environment also plays an important role. From the day you're born, everything about your surroundings and your lifestyle either enhances or detracts from your abilities.

. . . and with a good environment, you learn to play the hand well."

—Walter C. Alvarez

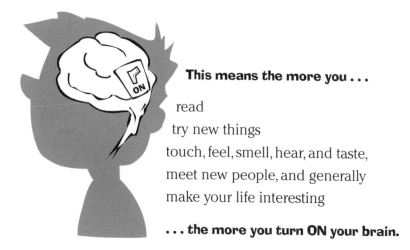

This means the more you . . .

read
try new things
touch, feel, smell, hear, and taste,
meet new people, and generally
make your life interesting

. . . the more you turn ON your brain.

On the other hand, if you avoid . . .

reading
trying new things
meeting new people
doing anything except watching TV, playing
video games, or otherwise limiting your life

**. . . you might
as well turn your
brain from
ON to OFF.**

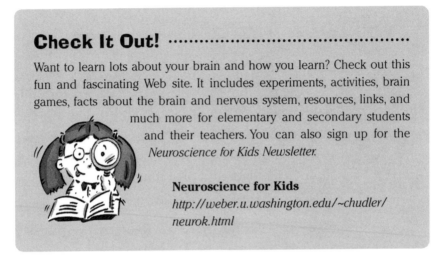

Check It Out! ··

Want to learn lots about your brain and how you learn? Check out this fun and fascinating Web site. It includes experiments, activities, brain games, facts about the brain and nervous system, resources, links, and much more for elementary and secondary students and their teachers. You can also sign up for the *Neuroscience for Kids Newsletter.*

Neuroscience for Kids
http://weber.u.washington.edu/~chudler/ neurok.html

4 Great Ways to Turn On Your Brain

1. Take classes outside of school. Check out libraries, community centers, recreation centers, and museums. See what they offer and sign up for something that interests you.

2. Start a book group with your friends. Decide each month on a book you'd all like to read. Set a deadline for reading it, then get together and talk about it. *Tip:* Visit a local library or bookstore for suggestions. Ask for publications or handouts about starting a book club.

3. Get a mentor. See page 69 for more on how to do this and why it's a good idea.

4. Go online. If you have access to a computer and the Internet, you've got the whole world at your fingertips. (If you don't have a computer at home or at school, ask at your local library about *free* community Internet access.)

Here are just a few recommended Web sites:

KidsWeb
http://www.npac.syr.edu/textbook/kidsweb/
Lots of links to sites about the arts, sciences, social studies, and other topics. A digital library for students in grades K–12.

Yahooligans!
http://www.yahooligans.com/
The Web guide for kids.

ExploraNet
http://www.exploratorium.edu/
The online version of San Francisco's popular museum of science, art, and human perception. Tons of fun and fascinating stuff.

Observatorium
http://observe.ivv.nasa.gov/
Explore NASA's big backyard with pictures and stories of the Earth, planets, and stars; space trivia; fun and games; and more.

A Kid's Guide to the Smithsonian
http://www.si.edu/resource/tours/kidsguide/
Go online for guided tours of the National Museum of Natural History, the National Museum of American History, and the National Air and Space Museum.

Tomorrow's Morning
1-800-AWARE-13 (1-800-292-7313)
Subscriptions: 1-800-607-4410
http://www.morning.com/
This lively weekly newspaper for kids ages 8–14 covers national and international news and entertaining features on science, the environment, nature, the stock market, and sports, plus brain teasers, contests, and more. Go online to read the current issue and the archives (back issues).

U.S. Geological Survey
http://info.er.usgs.gov/
Explore things on, in, around, and about the Earth including plants and animals, land, water, and maps. Learn how biology, geology, hydrology, and geography can help us understand our changing world. Tour the whole site or click on the Learning Web link for K–12 materials.

WebMuseum
http://sunsite.unc.edu/wm/
Look at and learn about hundreds of famous paintings, visit special exhibitions ...even take a tour of Paris!

The White House
http://www.whitehouse.gov/
Take a virtual tour, learn more about the U.S. government, email the President and Vice President, check out the White House for Kids pages, and more.

Check It Out! ••

There's an Internet email mailing list just for GTs. Subscribe (it's free!) to meet and communicate with other GTs, hook up with pen pals, and share

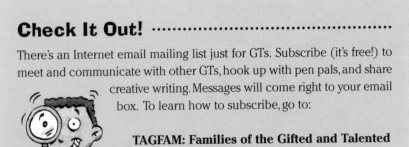

creative writing. Messages will come right to your email box. To learn how to subscribe, go to:

TAGFAM: Families of the Gifted and Talented
http://www.access.digex.net/~king/tagfam.html

When School Isn't Cool

One place where it should be easy to keep your brain turned ON is in school. Ironically, for many GTs, school is a definite turnOFF.

In my years of getting to know GTs, I've lost count of how many have told me:

Oh what a bore to sit and listen
To stuff we already know.
Do everything we've done and done again
But we still must sit and listen.
Over and over read one more page.
Oh bore,
Oh bore,
Oh bore.
Sometimes I feel if we do one more page
My head will explode with boreness rage.
I wish I could get up right there
And march right out the door.

—Girl, 9

From *Gifted Kids Speak Out* by James R. Delisle, © 1987. Free Spirit Publishing Inc., Minneapolis, MN; 800/735/7323. Used with permission.

While you may not feel this way about school all of the time, you probably feel this way some of the time. And when you do, it's nice to know that *you don't have to accept things the way they are.*

The first and most important step toward making school cool—meaning more challenging and interesting—is to know what you need to keep your brain turned ON. Nothing outrageous, just logical things like being able to:

✔ learn at your own speed, not someone else's
✔ pretest out of work you already know and understand
✔ study things you're interested in—beyond basic schoolwork
✔ work with ideas that really boggle your brain.

The second thing you'll need to do is help your teachers teach you better. Remember that teachers have students of varying abilities in their classes: slow learners, fast learners, kids with learning differences and other special needs. If you want school to be cool for you, it's up to *you* to take the initiative.* You don't have to stay stuck in the same-old-same-old. You can start being responsible for your own education...starting today.

---

* Talk with your parents and ask for their support. Tell them what's happening in school ... and what's not happening for you. Share the ideas on pages 47–51 with them. See if they're willing to back you up.

Last Resorts
12 Things GTs Do
When They're Bored Silly in School

1. Read.

2. Work ahead. (Sometimes without letting the teacher know.)

3. Draw or doodle.

4. Ask the teacher what to do.

5. Use the computer.

6. Play games.

7. Write.

8. Talk. (And try not to get caught.)

9. Help others with their schoolwork.

10. Do homework.

11. Fool around.

12. Twiddle their thumbs.

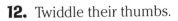

10 Ways to Make School More Cool*

1. Talk with your teachers about skipping over work you already know. This will free up time for more challenging projects. *Example:* Some kids take a pretest at the start of a spelling unit. If they score well on the pretest, they don't have to do the work for learning those words. (Why should they? They already know them.) You might apply this idea to other subjects, too.

2. Talk with your teachers about working independently. This is a great way to study subjects in more depth than regular classes usually allow. By working on your own thing, at your own speed, there's no limit to what you can learn. Ask your teacher to help you plan your study. Keep in mind that working *independently* doesn't necessarily mean working alone. GTs need help from others in learning the how-tos of independent study:

✔ What will you study and how?

> "Deciding on a project is hard 'cause you don't want to get bored with it—then you're stuck."
> —Jeff, 9

* Talk with your parents and ask for their support. Tell them what's happening in school…and what's not happening for you. Share these 10 ideas with them and see if they're willing to back you up.

✔ Who can help you? A librarian? Someone from the community?

✔ How long will it take?

✔ In what ways will you show what you've learned?
(*Tip:* See #9 on page 50.)

3. Talk with the special teachers in your school—those who teach art, music, dance, drama, creative writing, computers, and other subjects. Would they be willing to accept your help in planning activities and events?

4. Talk with your teachers about creating unique displays for your classroom or school. You could work on them alone or with other students. You might design a new display each month, and you'd be in charge of putting it up and taking it down. Here are two examples of displays produced by GTs I've talked to:

INVENTIONS AND INVENTORS. Enterprising and innovative GTs participated in an inventors' fair and made a display to coincide with the event. They included information about famous inventors as well as their own inventions.

COLLECTIONS. Collections make great displays, and most GTs I've known have had at least one. (The most unusual? Hundreds of different sugar packets from restaurants around the country!) Each display might include a brief description of the collection and information about how the collector got involved with it.

 THINK ABOUT IT: If you could start a collection that piqued your interest, what would it be? What would it look like? How would you tell others about your collection?

5. Talk with your teachers and principal about starting mini-classes for subjects not taught in your school. *Example:* If you'd like to learn a foreign language, find a few others who share your interest. Tell your teachers and principal about your idea. Ask them to help you figure out how, when, and where you could have your class. They might also be able to help you find a tutor. Borrow language tapes from the media center; add books and you're off. *C'est une bonne idée!*

6. Talk with your teachers about opting out of work you already know how to do. Doing double duty is a drag and a common glitch of gifted programs. GTs in special classes often get stuck doing all of the regular class assignments *and* the work for their gifted class. For some GTs, this isn't a problem. But for many others, the whole thing seems very unfair.

> *"For me, the main disadvantage of being GT is having to make up work that I miss when I go to my gifted class. Especially when I already know the stuff."*
> —Tara, 9

GTs shouldn't have to do more work or **MOTS*** work just because they're gifted. They should be allowed to do *different kinds of work.* Like some of the projects described here.

---

* **MOTS** = **M**ore **O**f **T**he **S**ame.

7. Volunteer to help your teachers in creative and productive ways. (Cleaning chalkboards or being the class gofer doesn't count.) Can you help plan units? Media centers and special teachers may welcome your energy and skills. Could you be a computer aid, a tutor, or a cable TV operator?

8. Start a journal. Write your thoughts, poetry, stories, doodles, movie reviews, new ideas, or other creative jottings in your spare time. According to the young author of *Totally Private & Personal: Journaling Ideas for Girls and Young Women:*

"There are only two rules for journal-keeping:
1. Date every entry.
2. Don't make any more rules."

—Jessica Wilber, 14

9. Ask your teachers if you can show what you learn in new and unusual ways. Instead of writing a report (if this is a big yawn for you), how about...

- making a diorama?
- giving an oral presentation?
- creating a slide show or photo essay?
- making a mobile?

- writing a play?
- composing a song?
- making a video?
- designing a Web page?
- _____?
  What's *your* idea?

10. Use your powers of persuasion to convince your teachers that you need an "any-time-of-the-day" library pass. *Be a regular customer of the media center* and learn as much as you can on your own. While teachers try to do their best, they're not going to be able to teach you everything you want to know.

> "The next best thing to knowing something is knowing where to find it."
> —Samuel Johnson

What If Your Teacher Says No?

OR

"Nope." • "No way." • "Sorry." • "Forget it." • "You can't do that." • "Nobody has ever done that before." • "If I let you do that, everyone else will want to do it, too." • "There's no time." • "I'm too busy." • "You already have enough to do." • "It's against the rules."

OR

"We can't make any more exceptions for you—you're already in the GT program."

? ? ? ? ? ? ?

Anyone who questions why things are done a certain way risks being resented by people who feel threatened by those questions. Anyone who suggests a different way of doing things risks rejection. As a GT, you need to recognize and accept that parents make mistakes, teachers make mistakes…and *you* make mistakes.

Teachers don't always know what's best for you. They may say no to your ideas. Or…they may say YES!!!!!

The point is: You won't know if you don't ask.

> *"The grown-ups' response, this time, was to advise me to lay aside my drawings of boa constrictors, whether from the inside or the outside, and devote myself instead to geography, history, arithmetic and grammar. That is why, at the age of six, I gave up what might have been a magnificent career as a painter. Grown-ups never understand anything by themselves, and it is tiresome for children to be always and forever explaining things to them."*
>
> – Antoine de Saint-Exupéry, *The Little Prince**

If you believe in yourself and your ideas, you need to be willing to take chances and keep trying, even though things won't always turn out the way you want them to. You may have to restructure what you're asking for so your teacher will be more likely to say yes. You may have to wait and ask again later. "No" might mean a firm "No"…or it might mean "Now is not the time to talk about this."

The point is: School won't be cool unless you do your part to make it that way.

---

* Excerpt from *The Little Prince* by Antoine de Saint-Exupéry, © 1943, 1971, by Harcourt Brace Jovanovich, Inc. Reprinted by permission of the publisher.

GTs Speak Out:
How do you feel when you can't work ahead in class?

"Mad."—*Girl, 9*

"Sad."—*Girl, 9*

"Bad."—*Girl, 8*

"Trapped."—*Girl, 10*

"Annoyed."—*Boy, 10*

"Punished."—*Boy, 12*

 "Grouchy."—*Boy, 10*

 "Held back."—*Boy, 11*

 "Bored, because we have a lot of slow learners in my class, and if they don't understand, my teacher explains and explains and explains...."—*Girl, 10*

 "Disappointed, because everyone has their own speed and we shouldn't all have to stay at the same pace."—*Boy, 12*

 "I feel that I'm not given a chance to live up to my potential."—*Boy, 12*

 "I feel like the teacher isn't even thinking of me."—*Boy, 10*

(Not Just) For Girls Only

Years ago, many GT girls were afraid to show their smarts. That's because most people thought that boys were supposed to be stronger, smarter, and better than girls. They figured that someday the girls (when they were women) would get married and stay home with the kids, while the boys (when they were men) worked and took care of them. So it wasn't that important for girls to succeed in school.

It's an old-fashioned idea, and one that we can

Kiss Goodbye!

Today, most people in the United States and some (but not all) other countries agree: It's great for girls to be smart. Both girls and boys have the right to a good education. Both girls (as women) and boys (as men) have the right to equal work for equal pay. Even *more* important, both have the right to make choices about their lives. Women can work and have careers; men can stay home with the kids.

Still, some girls try to hide the fact that they're GT. They may worry that boys won't like them if they use their brains. They may worry that other girls will think they're stuck-up or weird. They may worry that *nobody* will like them and they'll be all alone.

In the surveys taken to gather information for this book, more girls than boys said they were teased about being GT. More girls than boys said they worry about school.

There's something else you need to know if you're a girl.

Researchers have found that girls ages 8 and 9 are assertive, self-confident, and have high self-esteem. BUT...

Starting about age 11, girls' self-esteem starts to *fall.* Strong, self-confident girls become insecure about their feelings, abilities, and decisions. They focus on  how they look and how boys see them, which keeps them from competing at school. Their view of the future—and what's possible for them—becomes more limited.

Imagine that you're walking along a mountain path. You see a sign that says "WARNING! FALLING ROCKS!" What will you do? You'll be alert and watchful. You won't let a rock bonk you on the head.

You've just seen a sign that says "WARNING! FALLING SELF-ESTEEM!" What will you do? How will you protect yourself? How will you keep your self-esteem HIGH during those risky teen years?

Check It Out! ••

Girls Seen and Heard: 52 Life Lessons for Our Daughters by The Ms. Foundation for Women and Sondra Forsythe (New York: Jeremy P. Tarcher, 1998).

Make your voice heard, take control of your life, and invest in your future with help from this book. You'll learn to collaborate with others, network, negotiate, effect change, and rise to all of life's challenges. For girls ages 9–15.

(Not Just) For Boys Only

Researchers have found that:

• Teachers call on boys four times more often than they call on girls.

• They ask boys *more* challenging questions, girls *less* difficult questions.

• They are more likely to praise boys' *intellectual* contributions and girls' *socialization* skills—meaning they like it when boys are smart and girls are friendly.

• In general, teachers pay more attention to boys than to girls.

If you're a boy, it seems you've got it made at school. BUT...

If you're a GT boy, think again.

One study found that being GT is an advantage for elementary school *girls* but not for boys. Here are some possible reasons why:

• Most teachers are women who tend to value conformity and obedience. GT boys are more likely than GT girls to question authority, rebel, and be the class troublemakers.

• Girls grow up faster than boys. In general, boys mature more slowly, especially in the verbal and reading areas. Bright, active boys might be labeled "hyperactive," "distractible," or "disorderly."

When Kent State professor Jim Delisle and I surveyed GTs for our teen version of *The Gifted Kids' Survival Guide,* many teens reported that boys face special problems. Here are the Top Three:

#1 Being labeled a "nerd" and teased about being GT.

#2 Peer pressure to fit in and conform.

#3 High expectations, extra work, and/or more responsibility.

Plus there's pressure on boys to be macho—aggressive, competitive, and insensitive. Boys are taught to hide their feelings, not show them. And they're never, ever supposed to cry.

It's been said that the *least* popular kid in America is the gifted, nonathletic boy.

THINK ABOUT IT: Are boys and girls treated differently in your school? If they are, what can you do about it? (*Tip:* You can start by treating the people you know— boys *and* girls—fairly and respectfully.)

> "We need every human gift and cannot afford to neglect any gift because of artificial barriers of sex or race or class or national origin."
> —Margaret Mead

When You Can't Take the Teasing

According to GTs, one of the worst things about being gifted is the teasing that comes with the label. And there are no two ways about it: When you're GT, you *will* be teased.

For some GTs, teasing isn't a big deal. They're able to go on doing their own thing and don't really care what other people say.

But many others feel differently.

> "Teasing hurts, mentally and even physically at times."
> —Jeff, 9

Often, the teasing comes in the form of not-so-fun nicknames:

- Mr. Genius
- Ms. Know-It-All
- Wise Guy
- Hotshot
- Smarty Pants
- Bookworm
- Teacher's Pet
- Brain
- Einstein
- Hypo (short for HIGH POTENTIAL)
- _____

What have *you* been called?

grrr!

GTs Speak Out:

How do you get teased?

 "People say I have a big head."—*Boy, 11*

 "They think we are perfect and that we are snobs."—*Boy, 10*

 "People say 'You're gifted and you got a B?'"—*Boy, 7*

"I get teased about always having a book and reading so much. People say I'm a nerd."—*Girl, 10*

"People call me Big Brain."—*Boy, 9*

 "If I answer a lot of questions, they call me a 'think-you-know-it-all.'"—*Boy, 9*

 "People say 'Look, it's the computer that wears tennis shoes!'"—*Girl, 10*

How to Cope with Teasing

It helps to know some of the reasons *why* kids tease you. Here are a few possibilities:

• They may be jealous of you. They may wish *they* could do as well as you in school.

• They may feel inferior around you. They think teasing *you* will help them feel better about *themselves.*

• They may not like you.

• They may tease just for fun. *All* kids get teased about something. If you weren't being teased about being GT, you'd probably be teased about something else.

• If your friends are doing the teasing, they may not know a better way to say "I like you." Some people aren't very good at giving compliments.

No matter why you're getting teased, you need to decide:

 Are you going to let the teasing bug you?

The next time someone teases you for being smart or doing something well, ask yourself these three questions. Then see if you don't feel better about the situation.

1. Who's doing the teasing? Is that person's opinion important to me?

2. Why are they teasing me? Just for fun? Because they're jealous? Because they just plain don't like me?

3. Do I accept the teasing? Am I going to let it get me down? Or am I going to ignore it and go about my business?

If you automatically accept the teasing that comes your way, you're not in control of your feelings. Someone else (the teaser) is. And if you worry too much about what other kids say, you may never be able to do what you really want to do. You'll be too busy trying to please everyone else.

According to GTs who've been there, here's the *best* way to cope with teasing:

"Just ignore kids who tease, or laugh along if they're your friends. It's just not important enough to get all worked up about."

If that doesn't work for you, here's another way to handle touchy situations:

1. Take a deep breath while counting to three. Then slowly breathe out while counting to six. (This will help you relax so you can talk without sounding MAD.)

2. Stand straight and tall with both feet firmly on the ground.

3. Look the person in the eye and say how you feel about the teasing. *Examples:* "It makes me sad to hear that." "It makes me angry when people make fun of others." DON'T blame or tease back. That only causes *more* problems.

4. Ask for an apology or simply walk away.

By using your smarts, your words, your eyes, and your body language, you'll send a clear message: STOP THE TEASING.

Will the other person stop? Maybe … and maybe not. You can't control what someone else thinks, says, or does. You *can* control what YOU think, say, and do. The important thing to remember is: *You have a right to stick up for yourself and say what you feel.*

Getting Along GT

We all need friends—people to hang out with, have fun with, and talk to when we're feeling blue. We need people who are there for us and like us the way we are.

It's not always easy for GTs to find friends. No matter what you say or do, some people won't want to be friends with you. You can try and try and it won't make any difference. But guess what: This is true for *everyone*, not just GTs!

Over the years, I've asked many GTs to share their advice and insights on making and keeping friends. Here's what they have to say.

The Top 10 Friendship Tips from GTs Like You

1. Don't be a show-off. That's wrong and it won't get you any friends.

2. Help people see that you have other interests besides school-work. Let them know you're more than just a super speller or a math whiz. Find out about *their* interests, too. You may have a lot in common.

3. Get into a GT class if you can. You'll find other kids who think and learn the way you do.

4. Be respectful. Think about how other kids feel when you do things well. Compliment them when *they* do things well.

> "Treat your friends as you do your pictures and place them in their best light."
>
> —Jennie Jerome Churchill

5. Don't always try to have things your way. Be willing to com-promise.

6. Get involved in things outside of school—groups, activities, classes, and clubs where you'll meet new people who share your interests.

7. Be patient. When you're trying to teach or explain something to other kids and they don't get it right away, don't get aggravated. Take your time or try another way.

8. Don't feel weird about having friends who are older or younger than you.

> "The term 'peer' does not . . . mean people of the same age, but refers to individuals who can interact at an equal level around issues of common interest."
>
> —W. C. Roedell

9. Be a friend. Be kind, caring, honest, trustworthy, and a good listener.

10. When other kids ask you for help, don't feel bad about saying no. Sometimes you don't have time. Sometimes you just don't feel like helping. True friends will understand.

THINK ABOUT IT: If you could give one piece of advice to other GTs about making and keeping friends, what would it be? Would you (do you) follow your own advice?

> "Nobody can give you wiser advice than yourself."
>
> —Cicero

3 More Friendship Tips to Try

1. Ask your parents to help you connect with other GTs.
They might talk with your teachers or GT program teachers at
other schools. Or they might join the National Association of
Gifted Children (NAGC), or a state organization dedicated to helping gifted children. For more information about NAGC or other
organizations, see pages 91–92.

2. Get a pen pal. Here are three pen-pal organizations you can
contact:

International Pen Friends (IPF)
P.O. Box 290065
Brooklyn, NY 11229
1-800-789-4988
http://www.global-homebiz.com/ipf.html

Peace Pals
RR 1, Box 118
Benton Road
Wassaic, NY 12592
(914) 877-6093
http://members.aol.com/pforpeace/peacepals/

World Pen Pals
P.O. Box 337
Saugerties, NY 12477
(914) 246-7828

3. Get a mentor. A mentor is a caring adult who will guide you, encourage you, and join you in exploring your special interests. You might find a mentor

- in your neighborhood

- at school

- in your congregation

- at a recreation center or community center

- where your parents work

- at a youth service organization such as Big Brothers Big Sisters, the YMCA/YWCA, Boy Scouts, Girl Scouts, Boys Clubs, or Girls, Inc.

Check It Out! 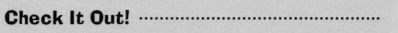

To learn *much* more about mentors and how to find one, contact:

One to One/The National Mentoring Partnership
2801 M Street NW
Washington, DC 20007
(202) 338-3844
http://www.mentoring.org/

GTs Speak Out:
On Friends and Friendship

How do you make friends?

 "I make friends by being a friend."—*Boy, 10*

 "I make friends by asking their name, and just talking, and being myself."—*Girl, 10*

 "I talk with them and then we build our relationship as we learn more about each other."—*Girl, 10*

 "I walk up to people and say hi. And maybe we have a conversation about a movie or a book or the disgusting school lunch. Then you talk and get to know each other."—*Girl, 10*

What is a good friend?

"Someone who cares about you, and helps you when you fall, and is there for you when you're mad, sad, or glad."—*Girl, 9*

"Someone who's understanding, honest, and knows how to make you feel better when things go wrong. Plus, they should know how to make you laugh or give sympathy."—*Girl, 12*

"A good friend never calls you names. They always stick up for you and they help you when you need it."—*Boy, 9*

"A good friend to me doesn't care how smart I am or how I look or if I win first place in a popularity contest. They listen and never keep secrets from you."—*Girl, 10*

"My friend doesn't care if I get all A's and she gets all C's. She's happy for me!"—*Girl, 9*

Growing Up GT

Some of the hassles you have at home are probably not much different than what other kids experience. Things like:

- whose turn it is to do the dishes and take out the trash
- not being able to consume unlimited quantities of junk food
- deciding who gets to watch his or her favorite TV program.

The list could go on and on.

But GTs have some hassles at home that most other kids don't have to deal with.

Great Expectations

"Sometimes my parents just expect too much of me. They want me to get A's in every subject."
—Andy, 9

Andy says he tries hard to do well in school, and he enjoys the challenge of working for A's. BUT he feels too much pressure when his parents tell him they want all A's all the time.

"My mom and dad expect me to be totally responsible for things around the house and not to play. They think it's a waste of time. I don't think that's fair."
—Kevin, 10

Kevin has a different kind of problem. His parents expect perfect behavior AND good grades!

What can YOU do when YOUR parents pressure YOU?

First, try to understand WHY your parents want you to do so well at everything. Here are some possible reasons:

• When you do well, they *feel* good. They're proud of you and your accomplishments.

• When you do well, they *look* good. Other people think they're doing a wonderful job of being parents.

• Parents hear a lot about GTs needing to "work up to their HIGH POTENTIAL." Your parents may think that if you're not getting A's, you're not learning as much as you should and could.

• GTs sometimes act more grown-up than other kids their age. Parents get used to these grown-up ways, and they start to expect that behavior all the time. So if you act goofy, kooky, or just want to have some fun, your parents may think you're being irresponsible. (Now *that's* a silly idea.)

Now that you know some reasons why parents have great expectations, you can try these ideas:

1. Talk with your parents about their high expectations.
Let them know how you feel. Angry? Uptight? Unhappy? Inadequate? Like you'll never be good enough for them?

Once your parents know how their expectations make you feel, they might be more likely to relax and try to accept you for who you are. If your parents aren't as understanding as you'd like, find another supportive adult—another relative, a teacher, a youth leader, or a neighbor.

2. Take it easy on yourself. GTs are often their own worst critics. They get in the habit of expecting so much of themselves that they become Nervous Nellies without any help from anyone else at all. Remember that it's all right to:

- flub up
- botch things
- make mistakes
- bomb out
- not be perfect (for more about this, see pages 81–83).

3. Remind your parents (in a nice way) that *they* don't always do their best and yet things usually turn out okay. Try to think of a time when you didn't do your best and still learned a lot or had fun. Ask your mom or dad to do the same.

> "My parents are satisfied if they know I worked hard on something, even if I didn't get an A."
> —Leslie, 11

Overcommitment

IF you have many different interests and abilities, and . . .

IF you're really good at some things and would like to be good at a lot of things, and . . .

IF your parents give you every possible opportunity to succeed . . .

THEN you might have another hassle common to GTs:

 Doing TOO MUCH.

Maybe Monday is scouts and Tuesday you've got gymnastics and Wednesday is your piano lesson and Thursday is your Spanish tutor and Friday is chess club and Saturday is softball and . . . HELP!!!!!

When do you have time for yourself?

If the answer is *never*, it's time to do something about it. You might try this:

1. Make a list of your commitments. Include everything—homework, chores, extracurricular activities, lessons, practice, clubs, etc. etc. etc.

2. Prioritize your list. Put a 1 by anything you *must* do—things that are non-negotiable. (*Example:* You can't *not* do your homework.) Put a 2 by anything you *love* to do. Put a 3 by anything you think you can do without.

3. Talk to your parents. See if they're willing to let you give up anything (everything?) you marked with a 3.

4. Try not to overcommit yourself in the future. It's important to leave time in your schedule to do...nothing. Time to be free, to relax, to chill out, to have fun, to sleep, to daydream.

Sibling Problems

"My brother is always trying to prove he's better than me and teases me about being a brain because I'm in the gifted class and he's not."

—Sara, 9

All brothers and sisters argue about things. It's natural, and it happens in every family.

But GTs run into double trouble when schoolwork is very easy for them and very hard for a brother or sister. Your siblings may be even more unhappy if you're chosen for the GT program and they're not.

Try these tips for keeping the peace:

• Remember that each person in your family is special in some way. You won't all be good at the same things. Be sure to let your brothers and sisters know what you like and appreciate about them. Recognize their talents and tell them when they do something well.

• If your brothers or sisters tease you about being a brain or being in the GT program, it's probably because they wish they were, too. Think about how *you* would feel if they were selected for the program and you weren't. A little empathy goes a long way.

• Be patient. Try to understand that people learn in different ways and at different times. Your brothers or sisters may need more help and time to do things than you. They're not perfect. *You're* not perfect.

Some GTs have another sibling problem: The Super-Over-Achieving Big Brother or Sister. This is the person who did *every-thing* right, from getting straight A's to winning awards to winning elections and leading clubs. And now *you're* expected to follow in those giant-sized footsteps.

Forget it! Just be yourself. If your parents compare you to your older SuperSibling, ask them (nicely) to please stop. Tell them how it makes you feel. If your teachers do the comparing, talk to them about it. Ask them to please see you as *you*, not as someone else's little brother or sister.

Feeling Like an Alien

A spaceship must have brought you to Earth when you were a baby. Because there's no other possible explanation for how you can be SO DIFFERENT from everyone else in your family!

If you sometimes feel this way... relax. It's not unusual for GTs to suddenly pop up in so-called "average" families. And maybe your family isn't average after all. It's possible that your parents and siblings have gifts that weren't encouraged or haven't been discovered.

If you really can't talk to anyone in your family—if they just don't understand you or what it means to be GT—find someone else to talk to. You might start with another relative, a teacher, a youth leader, or a neighbor. Or get a mentor. (See page 69.)

GTs Speak Out:

What's the best thing your parents do for you?

 "They tell me as long as I did my best they don't care what grade I get."—*Boy, 11*

 "They encourage me to keep going, and trying, and to fight my fears, and never give up."—*Girl, 10*

 "They tell me never to hold myself back, and always to be myself no matter what anyone else says."—*Girl, 10*

 "They praise me, and help me, and have fun with me."—*Girl, 10*

"They give me lots of hugs and tell me they love me a lot."—*Girl, 11*

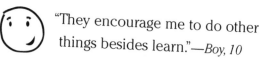 "They encourage me to do other things besides learn."—*Boy, 10*

 "They give me constructive criticism."—*Girl, 10*

 "They don't act weird around my friends."—*Boy, 12*

 "They just let me be me."—*Girl, 9*

 "Most of all they love me no matter how much I screw up."—*Boy, 10*

The Perfection Infection (and Cure)

GTs are especially susceptible to the Perfection Infection. When they get it, they find it nearly impossible to accept anything done imperfectly.

Perfect papers are IN. Imperfect papers are OUT. Drawings with minor mistakes end up in the wastebasket. Projects with defects (no matter how small) are started over.

This is a frustrating way to live.

It's not hard to understand how GTs catch the Perfection Infection. Parents, teachers, and even friends often expect them to be flawless and faultless.

"When we have tests, people make bets to see if I'll get everything right. Then, if I don't get a perfect paper, they say 'If you're smart, how come you got some wrong?'"
—Colleen, 9

"A lot of people think that just because I'm good at some things, I should be good at everything."
—John, 10

GTs who believe this blather may:

- start feeling inferior
- start believing that nothing they do is ever good enough
- start doing things simply to please others instead of doing them because they want to
- stop trying new things for fear of not being able to do them perfectly.

What can you do if you've got the bug? Tell yourself the Three Great Truths About Perfectionism:

1. Nobody's perfect, and no one is good at everything.
Albert Einstein was one of the world's greatest scientists, yet he didn't learn to read until he was 7. Learn to give the things that are

most important to you your maximum amount of energy. Then give yourself a break and don't go all out in everything else.

2. It's perfectly okay to be perfectly imperfect! You've probably heard this before, but it's worth repeating: *We learn best from our mistakes.* People who never take chances because they're afraid to make mistakes don't learn as much as those who do. (They don't have much fun, either.)

> "Every human being has the right to make FOUR BIG MISTAKES every day."
> —Gershen Kaufman and Lev Raphael

3. Doing things perfectly doesn't make you a more successful person. Other things count, too. Getting an A in math or reading doesn't mean you're a nicer person, only smarter in math or reading. It's healthy to spend at least some of your energy learning to care about and help others.

> "The principal mark of genius is not perfection but originality, the opening of new frontiers."
> —Arthur Koestler

Feeling Free to Be GT

In this book, you've been reading about making changes and taking charge of your life. It's time to ask yourself: *Do you have the guts to do it?*

How can you avoid getting weak in the knees when you go to negotiate with your parents or teachers? How can you be assertive so you get what you need? How can you stick up for your rights?

What *are* your rights, anyway?

**8 Great
Rights of
Gifted Kids**

1. You have a right to live WITHOUT the 8 Great Gripes. (See page 4.)

2. You have a right to be in classes that are challenging and interesting (not just **MOTS***).

3. You have a right to know about giftedness and why you're in (or should be in) a GT program or class.

4. You have a right to make mistakes and not do your best all the time.

5. You have a right to be with other kids who really understand you.

6. You have a right to be treated with respect by your friends, teachers, and parents.

7. You have a right to be different.

8. You have a right to stick up for your rights.

While none of these rights seems outrageous—and all of them make sense—many GTs don't have them.

---

* **MOTS** = **M**ore **O**f **T**he **S**ame.

"If you don't ask, you don't get."
—Mohandas Gandhi

It's up to YOU to see that you get your rights. When you go to your teachers to ask for changes in school, or when you talk with your parents about things that concern you, keep these Do's and Don'ts in mind:

DO

1. Know what you want changed *before* you meet with your teachers or parents. Try to have as many facts to back up your request as possible.

2. Try to think about the other person's position—and how he or she feels—so you can anticipate any possible objections.

3. Pick a good time and place for your meeting. (Obviously if there's chaos in the classroom, or your parents are very busy, it's *not* the right time. You might want to ask when it would be a good time to talk.)

4. Start with a small request so you're more likely to succeed. Then work up to bigger things once you've shown you can handle responsibility.

"You can't achieve anything without getting in someone's way."
—Abba Eban

DON'T

1. Wait. You can start learning how to be assertive right now.

2. Blame people. It doesn't help.

3. Refuse to compromise. If you give a little, others are more likely to give, too.

4. Stop trying. If at first you don't succeed, try again . . . or try another way.

> *"Patience is a necessary ingredient of genius."*
> —Benjamin Disraeli

Check It Out!

Stick Up For Yourself: Every Kid's Guide to Personal Power and Positive Self-Esteem by Gershen Kaufman, Ph.D., and Lev Raphael, Ph.D. (Minneapolis: Free Spirit Publishing, 1990). How to stick up for yourself with other kids, older siblings, even parents and teachers.

A Few Final Words

"It's not easy being green."
—Kermit the Frog

It's not always easy being GT. But I hope this book has made it a little easier for you. You know now that (1) you're not alone, (2) you have rights, and (3) you can stick up for your rights.

I hope you'll be free to be all you can be…and have fun along the way.

Resources for Parents and Teachers

Alvino, James. *Parents' Guide to Raising a Gifted Child* (New York: Ballantine Books, 1996). This practical guide to raising and educating gifted children includes advice on selecting the best day care or school, offers tips on promoting intellectual and creative-thinking abilities and research skills, and lists the best resources available for gifted kids.

Cheney, Martha C. *How To Develop Your Child's Gifts and Talents in Reading* (Los Angeles: Contemporary Books, 1996). This how-to book helps parents enrich their children's reading experiences by strengthening critical thinking, reading and comprehension, and vocabulary skills. Includes a list of recommended books.
—*How To Develop Your Child's Gifts and Talents in Vocabulary* (Los Angeles: Lowell House, 1997). A helpful and inventive guide to building up a child's storehouse of words.
—*How To Develop Your Child's Gifts and Talents in Writing* (Los Angeles: Lowell House, 1997). Begins with the basics—words, sentences, and paragraphs—and helps young writers create and develop poems, stories, reports, and essays.

Clark, Barbara C. *Growing Up Gifted: Developing the Potential of Children at Home and at School* (New York: Merrill, 1997). One of the most interesting, information-packed introductions available to the characteristics of gifted and talented children.

Halsted, Judith Wynn. *Some of My Best Friends Are Books: Guiding Gifted Readers from Preschool to High School* (Scottsdale, AZ: Gifted Psychology Press, 1995). Lists more than 300 books that address both the emotional and intellectual needs of gifted kids. Each entry is annotated, summarized, and organized by age and topic. Also includes guided discussions.

Rimm, Sylvia, Ph.D. *Keys to Parenting the Gifted Child* (Hauppauge, NY: Barrons Educational Series, 1994). How to work with schools, manage problems, and act as an advocate for your child.

Smutney, Joan Franklin, M.A., Sally Yahnke Walker, Ph.D., and Elizabeth A. Meckstroth, M.Ed. *Teaching Young Gifted Children in the Regular Classroom: Identifying, Nurturing, and Challenging Ages 4–9* (Minneapolis: Free Spirit Publishing, 1997). Written for educators (and parents) who believe that all children deserve the best education we can give them.

Walker, Sally Yahnke. *The Survival Guide for Parents of Gifted Kids: How to Understand, Live With, and Stick Up For Your Gifted Child* (Minneapolis: Free Spirit Publishing, 1991). The parents' companion to this *Gifted Kids' Survival Guide* explains what giftedness means, how kids are identified as gifted, how to advocate for your child at school, and more.

Webb, James T., Elizabeth Meckstroth, and Stephanie S. Tolan. *Guiding the Gifted Child: A Practical Source for Parents and Teachers* (Scottsdale, AZ: Gifted Psychology Press, 1989). A classic, packed with parenting techniques and information to help you identify the uniqueness of your gifted and talented child.

Winebrenner, Susan. *Teaching Gifted Kids in the Regular Classroom: Strategies and Techniques Every Teacher Can Use to Meet the Academic Needs of the Gifted and Talented* (Minneapolis: Free Spirit Publishing, 1992). Read this to learn about many ways to meet the learning needs of gifted students in the mixed-abilities classroom. Then pass it on to your child's teacher.

Winner, Ellen. *Gifted Children: Myths and Realities* (New York: Basic Books, 1997). A professor of psychology examines the latest scientific evidence about the biological basis of giftedness, as well as the role played by parents and schools in fostering exceptional abilities.

Yablun, Ronn. *How to Develop Your Child's Gifts and Talents in Math* (Los Angeles: Lowell House, 1995). Exercises, tips, and examples help children of all ages grasp math concepts and applications.

Organizations

The Association for the Gifted (TAG)
The Council for Exceptional Children (CEC)
1920 Association Drive
Reston, VA 20191-1589
1-888-CDC-SPED (1-888-232-7733)
http://www.cec.sped.org/
Provides information to professionals and parents about gifted and talented children and their needs. TAG is a division of CEC, and you must be a CEC member to participate. Members receive the *Journal for the Education of the Gifted* and the *TAG Update* newsletter, each quarterly. *Note:* If you visit the CEC Web site, click on Eric Clearinghouse on Disabilities and Gifted Education, then on Gifted Education for a directory of Frequently Asked Questions (FAQs) files, digest, fact sheets, and links. This is academic reading but worth it if you're interested.

National Association for Gifted Children (NAGC)
1701 L Street NW, Suite 550
Washington, DC 20036
(202) 785-4268
http://www.nagc.org/
A national advocacy group of parents, educators, and affiliate groups united in support of gifted education. Join to receive the quarterly magazine *Parenting for High Potential,* discounts on selected NAGC publications, and more. NAGC has affiliates in nearly every state.

Supporting the Emotional Needs of the Gifted (SENG)
405 White Hall
Kent State University
P.O. Box 5190
Kent, OH 44242-0001
(330) 672-4450
http://monster.educ.kent.edu/CoE/EFSS/SENG/
Directed by Dr. James R. Delisle and Dr. James T. Webb, this respected organization helps parents identify giftedness in their children and provides guidance, information, and resources that help children come to understand and accept

their unique talents. It also provides a forum for parents and educators to communicate about effective ways to live and work with gifted individuals. Members receive special publications about giftedness, a tri-annual newsletter, discounts for publications and the annual SENG conference, and a membership card. Request an application by calling (330) 672-3237.

Web Sites

David C. Baird's Gifted Children Web Site
http://home.ican.net/~agtechn/
A collection of thoughts and advice from people who have spent years identifying the gifted, working with them, and helping them define themselves, their strengths, and their role in society.

Gifted and Talented (TAG) Resources Home Page
http://www.eskimo.com/~user/kids.html
This comprehensive collection includes links to all known online gifted resources, enrichment programs, talent searches, summer programs, gifted mailing lists, early acceptance programs, years' worth of mailing list archives, and information for many local gifted associations and government (mostly U.S. state) programs.

The Gifted Child Society
http://www.gifted.org/
This nonprofit organization provides educational enrichment and support services for gifted children, assistance to parents, and training for educators. Since 1957, the Society has served over 50,000 children and their families. In 1975, the U.S. Department of Education named it a national demonstration model.

Gifted Children
http://www.gifted-children.com/
Gifted Children Monthly, a multi-award-winning newsletter "for the parents of children of great promise," has ceased publication—and returned as *Gifted-Children.com,* a networking and information site. Members have access to news, articles, archives, resources, downloadable files, a chat and BBS forum network, and more. Join online.

GT World
http://www.gtworld.org/
This online support community for parents of gifted and talented children offers articles, links, testing information, definitions, three mailing lists, and a MOO where members can talk to each other in real time.

The Hoagies' Gifted Education Page
http://www.ocsc.com/hoagies/gift.htm
A wide variety of resources for parents and educators of gifted youth, from research to everyday success stories, personal support groups, and links.

TAG Family Network
http://www.teleport.com/~rkaltwas/tag
Run by and for parents, this organization is dedicated to appropriate education and advocacy for gifted and talented youth. It disseminates information, supports parents, and monitors and influences legal issues. The Web site contains current information on gifted education with links to many other sites of interest to parents, educators, and children. Membership is free; to join, fill out the online membership form.

TAGFAM: Families of the Gifted and Talented
http://www.access.digex.net/~king/tagfam.html
An Internet-based support community for talented and gifted individuals and their families. Read the interesting articles and join one (or more) of the five TAG project mailing lists: TAGFORUM (discussions, debates, and advocacy education); TAGFAM (parenting education and an online support group); TAGMAX (for parents who have decided to be directly responsible for their gifted children's learning and education, whether through full-time home schooling or as a supplement to regular schooling); TAGKIDS (where gifted children share their creative writing, hook up with pen pals, and more); and TAGTEENS (general discussion for gifted teens and college students, run for teens by teens).

Index

About the Author

 Judy Galbraith, M.A., has a master's degree in guidance and counseling of the gifted and has worked with and taught gifted youth, their parents, and their teachers for over ten years. In 1983, she started Free Spirit Publishing, which specializes in SELF-HELP FOR KIDS® and SELF-HELP FOR TEENS.®

Judy is also the coauthor of *The Gifted Kids' Survival Guide: A Teen Handbook* (with Jim Delisle, Ph.D.), *Managing the Social and Emotional Needs of the Gifted* (with Connie Schmitz, Ph.D.), *What Kids Need to Succeed: Proven, Practical Ways to Raise Good Kids* (with Peter L. Benson, Ph.D., and Pamela Espeland), and *What Teens Need to Succeed: Proven, Practical Ways to Shape Your Own Future* (with Peter and Pamela).

Judy lives in Minneapolis, Minnesota, with Chloé, her comic Airedale "terror." She recently achieved a major life goal: building a house on Madeline Island in Lake Superior. Her future goals include getting her captain's license (for sailing) and renovating a historic office building.

Other Great Books from Free Spirit

How To Do Homework Without Throwing Up
by Trevor Romain
Trevor Romain understands how horrible homework can be. Kids will recognize this right away—and as they laugh along with Trevor's jokes, they'll learn how to make a homework schedule, when to do the hardest homework (first!), the benefits of homework, and more. For ages 8–13.
$8.95; 72 pp.; softcover; illus.; 5⅛" x 7"

Stick Up for Yourself!
Every Kid's Guide to Personal Power and Positive Self-Esteem
by Gershen Kaufman, Ph.D., and Lev Raphael, Ph.D.
Realistic, encouraging how-to advice for kids on being assertive, building relationships, becoming responsible, making good choices, solving problems, and more. For ages 8–12.
$9.95; 96 pp.; softcover; illus.; 6" x 9"

The Gifted Kids' Survival Guide
A Teen Handbook
Revised, Expanded, and Updated Edition
by Judy Galbraith, M.A., and Jim Delisle, Ph.D.
Vital information on giftedness, IQ, school success, college planning, stress, perfectionism, and much more. For ages 11–18.
$14.95; 304 pp.; softcover; illus.; 7¼" x 9¼"

Psychology for Kids
40 Fun Tests That Help You Learn About Yourself
by Jonni Kincher
Based on sound psychological concepts, these fascinating tests promote self-discovery, self-awareness, and self-esteem and empower young people to make good choices. For ages 10 & up.
$14.95; 152 pp.; softcover; illus.; 8½" x 11"

*To place an order or to request a free catalog of SELF–HELP FOR KIDS®
materials, please write, call, email, or visit our Web site:*

Free Spirit Publishing Inc.
400 First Avenue North • Suite 616 • Minneapolis, MN 55401-1724
toll-free 800.735.7323 • local 612.338.2068 • fax 612.337.5050
help4kids@freespirit.com • www.freespirit.com

The Gifted Kids' Survival Guide

For Ages 10 & Under

Revised & Updated Edition

If you're GT (Gifted and Talented), you've got lots of important questions about why you think and learn the way you do: faster, with more intensity and drive than many kids your age. Questions like: What does "gifted" mean? Who gets into gifted programs, and how? Why other kids tease you about being smart, and what can you do about it? How can you make school more challenging and interesting?

Hundreds of gifted kids contributed to this book, and they had plenty to say about growing up GT. Their advice and insights can help you know you're not alone, you're not "weird," and being smart, creative, and talented is a bonus, not a burden.

Look inside to find:

- 8 Great Gripes of Gifted Kids
- 8 Great Things About Being GT
- 8 Great Rights of Gifted Kids (and how to stick up for them)
- 10 Ways to Make School More Cool
- The Perfection Infection (and Cure)
- 4 Great Ways to Turn On Your Brain
- Smart Ways to Make and Keep Good Friends
- How to Handle Hassles at Home
- How to Be the Best You Can Be
- and *much* more

Judy Galbraith, M.A., has a master's degree in guidance and counseling of the gifted and has worked with and taught gifted youth, their parents, and their teachers for over ten years. In 1983, she started Free Spirit Publishing, which specializes in self-help books for kids and teens.

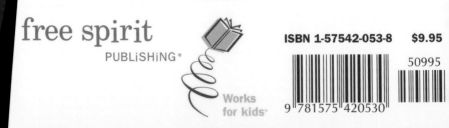

free spirit
PUBLISHING®

Works for kids®

ISBN 1-57542-053-8   **$9.95**

50995

9 781575 420530